PIANO • VOCAL • GUITAR

T0041546

TOP HITS OF 2022

EIGHTEEN OF THE YEAR'S BEST SONGS

ISBN 978-1-70517-631-3

Hal•Leonard®

Visit Hal Leonard Online at
www.halleonard.com

World headquarters, contact:
Hal Leonard
7777 West Bluemound Road
Milwaukee, WI 53213
Email: info@halleonard.com

In Europe, contact:
Hal Leonard Europe Limited
1 Red Place
London, W1K 6PL
Email: info@halleonardeurope.com

In Australia, contact:
Hal Leonard Australia Pty. Ltd.
4 Lentara Court
Cheltenham, Victoria, 3192 Australia
Email: info@halleonard.com.au

FREEDOM

Words and Music by TIERCE PERSON,
AUTUMN ROWE, ANDRAE ALEXANDER
and JONATHAN BATISTE

B♭

I hear a song ___ that takes me back, and I let go with so ___ much

F ... **C**

free - dom. ___ Free to live ___ (how I wan - na live). I'm 'on' get

B♭ ... **Fm**

(what I'm gon - na get), 'cause it's my free - dom. ___

___ The rea - son we get down ___ is to get back up. ___ If some - one's a - round ___

go on, ___ let them look. ___ You can't stand still, ___ this ain't no drill. ___

More than cheap thrills. _ Now is your time, _

__ (it's your right) you can shine ___ (it's al - right). _ If you do, ___ I'm - a do too. __

'Cause when I look up to the stars,

With pedal

* Lead vocal written an octave higher.

Lead vocal written at recorded pitch.

ABOUT DAMN TIME

Words and Music by LIZZO,
ERIC FREDERIC, THERON MAKIEL THOMAS,
LARRY PRICE, RONALD LARKINS,
STEPHEN HAGUE, BLAKE SLATKIN
and MALCOLM McLAREN

*Recorded a half step lower.

Bitch!

'Cause, uh, ___ you know what time it is, ___ uh.

I'm com - ing out to - night, ___ I'm com - ing out to - night. ___

I'm com - ing out to - night, ___ I'm com - ing out to - night. ___

AS IT WAS

Words and Music by HARRY STYLES,
THOMAS HULL and TYLER JOHNSON

You know ___ it's not the same as ___ it was, as ___ it was, ___ as ___ it was. ___

You know ___ it's not the same.

BAM BAM

Words and Music by CAMILA CABELLO,
ED SHEERAN, SCOTT HARRIS,
ERIC FREDERIC, EDGAR BARRERA
AND CHECHE ALARA

Syncopated Acoustic Pop

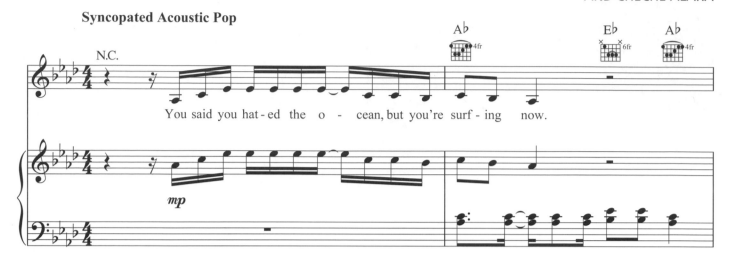

You said you hat-ed the o - cean, but you're surf-ing now.

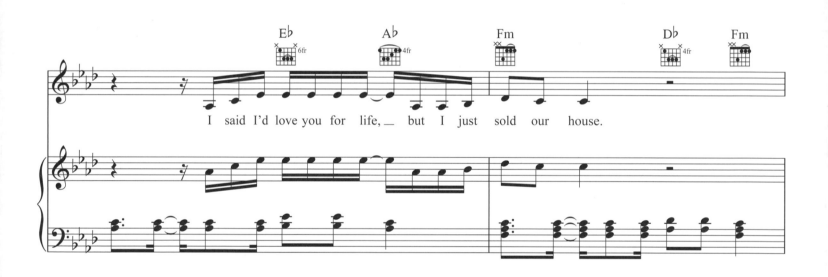

I said I'd love you for life, __ but I just sold our house.

We were kids at the start, __ I guess we're grown - ups now.

BOTH SIDES NOW

Words and Music by
JONI MITCHELL

Thoughtful, gentle

Bows and flows of an - gel hair, ___ and ice cream cas - tles

in the air, ___ and feath - er _____ can - yons ___ ev -'ry - where:

I've looked at clouds that way. But now they on - ly

*Recorded a half step lower.

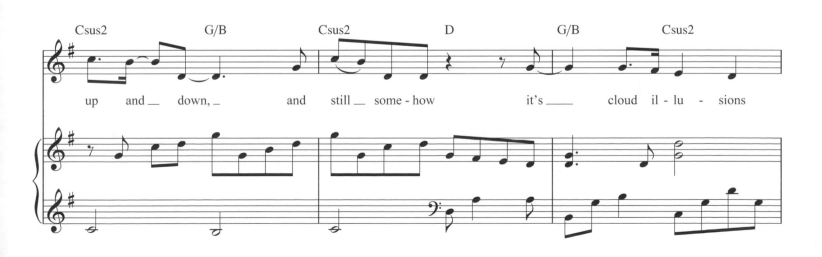

CAROLINA
from WHERE THE CRAWDADS SING

Words and Music by
TAYLOR SWIFT

Slowly, in 2

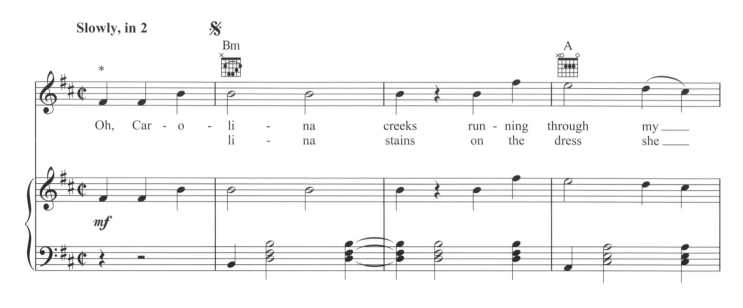

Oh, Car - o - li - na creeks run - ning through my ___ veins.
li - na stains on the dress my she ___ left.

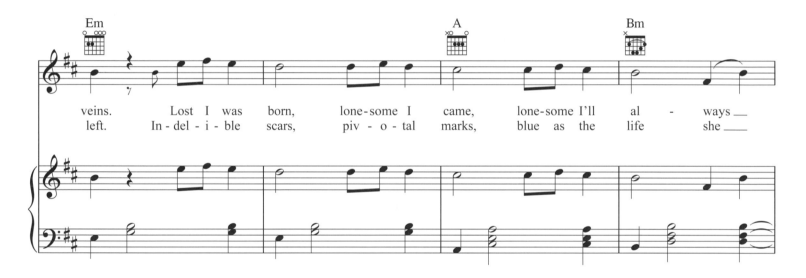

Lost I was born, lone - some I came, lone - some I'll al - ways ___ stay.
In - del - i - ble scars, piv - o - tal marks, blue as the life she ___ fled.

Car - o - li - na knows why, for years, I ___
Car - o - li - na pines, won't you cov - er ___

* Vocal line written one octave higher than sung.

To Coda

D.S. al Coda

ENEMY

Words and Music by DANIEL COULTER REYNOLDS,
DANIEL WAYNE SERMON, BENJAMIN ARTHUR McKEE,
DANIEL JAMES PLATZMAN, JUSTIN TRANTER,
MATTIAS LARSSON and ROBIN FREDRIKSSON

Rap: *(See additional lyrics)*

Additional Lyrics

Rap: Uh, look, okay
I'm hopin' that somebody pray for me
I'm prayin' that somebody hope for me
I'm stayin' where nobody 'posed to be
P-p-posted
Being a wreck of emotions
Ready to go whenever, just let me know
The road is long, so put the pedal into the floor
The enemy on my trail, my energy unavailable
I'm-a tell 'em, "Hasta luego"
They wanna plot on my trot to the top
I been outta shape thinkin' out the box, I'm an astronaut
I blasted off the planet rock to cause catastrophe
And it matters more because I had it not
Had I thought about wreaking havoc
On an opposition, kinda shockin' they wanted static
With precision, I'm automatic quarterback
I ain't talkin' sackin', pack it
Pack it up, I don't panic, batter-batter up
Who the baddest? It don't matter 'cause we at your throat

GLIMPSE OF US

Words and Music by JOJI KUSUNOKI,
CONNOR McDONOUGH, RILEY McDONOUGH,
JOEL CASTILLO and ALEXIS KESSELMAN

HOLD MY HAND

from TOP GUN: MAVERICK

Words and Music by STEFANI GERMANOTTA
and MICHAEL TUCKER

Power Ballad

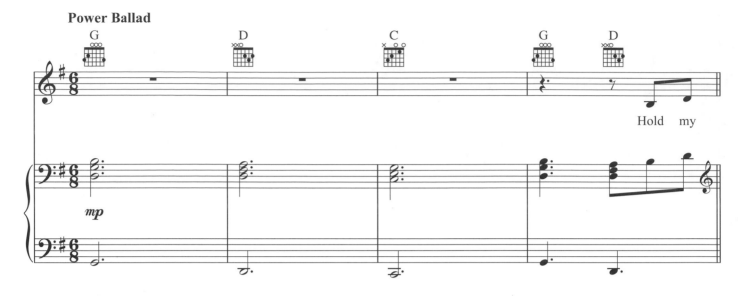

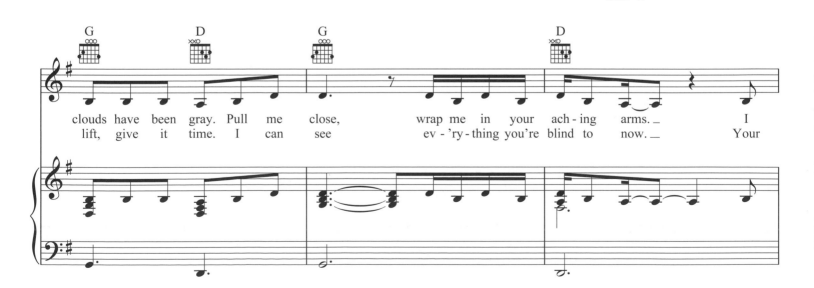

IN THE STARS

Words and Music by BENSON BOONE,
MICHAEL POLLACK and JASON EVIGAN

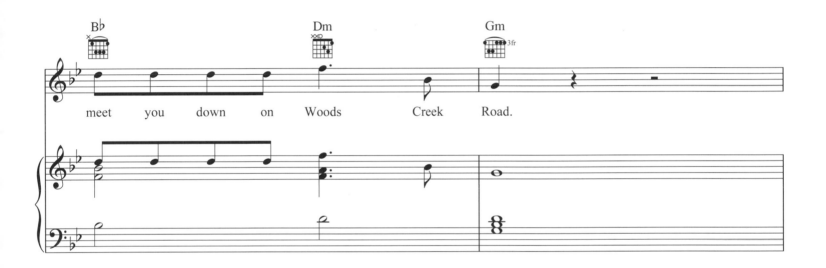

LIGHT SWITCH

Words and Music by CHARLIE PUTH,
JACOB KASHER HINDLIN and JACOB TORREY

Yeah.

Why you call-ing at e-lev-en thir-ty, when you
Do you love it when you keep me guess-ing when you're

on-ly wan-na do me dirt-y? But I
leav-ing, then you leave me stress-ing? But I

Recorded a half step higher.

LOVE ME MORE

Words and Music by SAM SMITH,
TOR HERMANSEN, JAMES NAPIER
and MIKKEL ERIKSEN

NUMB LITTLE BUG

Words and Music by EMILY BEIHOLD,
NICHOLAS LOPEZ and ANDREW DeCARO

Recorded a half step lower.

NOBODY LIKE U
from TURNING RED

Music and Lyrics by BILLIE EILISH
and FINNEAS O'CONNELL

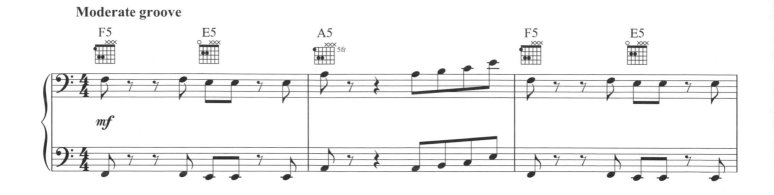

I've nev-er met no-bod-y ___ like ___ you. Had friends and I've had

bud-dies, ___ it's ___ true. ___ But they don't turn my tum-my ___ the way ___ you ___

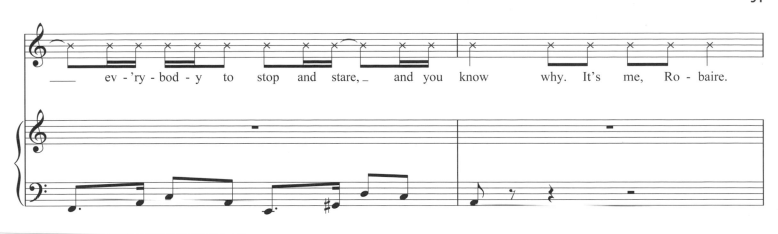

ev-'ry-bod-y to stop and stare,___ and you know why. It's me, Ro-baire.

Woo,   uhh,   let's

go.   You're nev-er not on my   right.

D.S. al Coda

CODA Am

N.C.

Li, li, li,   li,   li, like you.   Li, li, li,   li,   li, like you.

'TIL YOU CAN'T

Words and Music by BEN STENNIS
and MATT ROGERS

Country Rock, in 2

You can tell your old ___ man you'll
keep put - ting ___ off for -

do some large - mouth fish - ing an - oth - er time. ___ You just ___
ev - er with ___ that girl ___ whose heart you hold, ___ swear-

___ got too ___ much on ___ your plate ___ to bait and cast ___ a line.
- ing that ___ you'll ask ___ some - day ___ fur - ther down ___ the road. ___

* *Recorded a half step lower.*

Oh, if you got a chance, _____ take ___ it, take _
_ it while you got a chance. _ If you got a dream, _____ chase _
_ it 'cause a dream _ won't chase you back. _ If you're gon - na love _
_ some - bod - y, hold ___ them as long ___ and as strong ___ and as close ___ as you can _

ON MY WAY

from MARRY ME

Words and Music by LEROY JAMES CLAMPITT,
IVY ADARA and MICHAEL POLLACK

RUNNING UP THAT HILL

featured in the fourth season of the Netflix series STRANGER THINGS

Words and Music by
KATE BUSH

It does-n't hurt ___ me. D'you wan-na feel ___ how it feels? ___

UNTIL I FOUND YOU

Words and Music by EMILY BEIHOLD
and STEPHEN SANCHEZ

gain like I did. Oh, I used to _____ say I would

I would nev - er fall in love a - gain un - til